Medical Vocabulary for Interpreters

Essential English-Spanish **MEDICAL** Terms

José Luis Leyva

Series: Essential Technical Terminology

ISBN: 1985347326
ISBN-13: 978-1985347328

PREFACE

Being bilingual is an asset; and mastering different fields of speciality will make a difference in your bilingual skills. This book can be a helpful resource to learn the essential English-Spanish MEDICAL terms. Learn 4 to 5 terms each day and at the end of 2018 you will master the essential MEDICAL terminology in this language combination. This book contains only the most frequently used MEDICAL terminology in English and Spanish.

PREFACIO

Hablar dos idiomas es una gran ventaja; dominar diferentes campos de especialización marcará una diferencia es sus habilidades bilingües. Este libro puede ser de gran ayuda para aprender los términos MÉDICOS esenciales en inglés y español. Aprenda 4 ó 5 términos cada día y al final del 2018 usted habrá dominado la terminología MÉDICA esencial en esta combinación de idiomas. Este libro contiene solamente la terminología MÉDICA más frecuentemente utilizada en inglés y español.

A

abdomen, abdomen

abdominal, abdominal

abnormal, anormal

abortion, aborto

abrasion, abrasión/raspadura

abscess, absceso

abstinence, abstinencia

abuse, abuso

accident, accidente

acetaminophen, acetaminofén

ache, dolor

acid, ácido

acne, acné

active, activo

acute, agudo

addict, adicto

addiction, adicción

admit (into hospital), ingresar

adolescence, adolescencia

adopt (to), adoptar

adult, adulto

adrenaline, adrenalina

advise (to), aconsejar

afterbirth, placenta

agitation, agitación

ailment, enfermedad

air, aire

alcoholism, alcoholismo

alive, vivo

allergic, alérgico

allergy, alergia

ambulance, ambulancia

amenorrhea, amenorrea

amino acid, aminoácido

ammonia, amoníaco

amnesia, amnesia

amniocentesis, amniocentesis

amniotic sac, bolsa amniótica

amphetamines, anfetaminas

amputate (to), amputar

analgesic, analgésico

analysis, análisis

anaphylactic, shock anafiláctico

anatomy, anatomía

anemia, anemia

anemic, anémico

anesthesia, anestesia

anesthesiologist, anestesiólogo

aneurysm/aneurism, aneurisma

anger, enojo

angiogram, angiograma

angioplasty, angioplastia

anorexia, anorexia

antacid, antiácido

anthrax, ántrax

antibiotic, antibiótico

antibodies, anticuerpos

anticoagulant, anticoagulante

antidepressant, antidepresivo

antidote, antídoto

antihistamine, antihistamínico

anus, ano

anxiety, ansiedad

aorta, aorta

apathy, apatía

apnea, apnea

appendectomy, apendectomía

appendicitis, apendicitis

appetite, apetito

applicator, aplicador

appointment, cita

arm, brazo

arm pit, axila

arrhythmia, arritmia

artery, arteria

arthritis, artritis

asphyxia, asfixia

asthma, asma

asthmatic, asmático

astigmatism, astigmatismo

athlete's foot, pie de atleta

atrophy, atrofia

autism, autismo

autopsy, autopsia

awake, despierto

awaken (to), despertar

B

baby, bebé

back, espalda

backbone, columna vertebral

bacteria, bacteria

bad, malo(a)

balance, equilibrio

bald, calvo

baldness, calvicie

bandage, vendaje

bandaid, curita

barbiturates, barbitúricos

barium, bario

basin, palangana

bath, baño

bathe (to), bañarse

bed, cama

bedpan, orinal

bedridden (patient), encamado

bed-wetting, enuresis

behavior, conducta

belch, eructo

belly, vientre

bellybutton, ombligo

benign, benigno

bib, babero

biceps, bíceps

bicuspid, bicúspide

bile, bilis

bilirubin, bilirrubina

biological, biológico

biopsy, biopsia

birth, nacimiento/parto

birthmark, lunar

bite, mordedura

bite (insect), picadura

bitter, amargo

blackheads, espinillas

bladder, vejiga

bleed, sangrar

blind, ciego

blindness, ceguera

blink, parpadear

blister, ampolla

blockage, obstrucción

blood, sangre

body, cuerpo

bone, hueso

booster shot, vacuna de refuerzo

bottle, botella

botulism, botulismo

bowel, intestino

brace, aparato ortopédico

braces (dental), frenos dentales

brain, cerebro

break, quebrar

breast/chest, pecho/seno

breastbone, esternón

breath, aliento

breathe, respirar

broken, roto

bronchitis, bronquitis

bruise, moretón

bruised, amoratado

bulimia, bulimia

bulimic, bulímico

bump, protuberancia

bunion, juanete

burn, quemadura

burp, eructar

bursitis, bursitis

buttock, glúteo

buzzing, zumbido

C

calcified, calcificado

calcium, calcio

calf (of leg), pantorilla

callus, callo

calorie, caloría

cancer, cáncer

cancerous, canceroso

cane, bastón

capillary, capilar

capsule, cápsula

carbohydrate, carbohidrato

carcinogenic, carcinogénico

carcinoma, carcinoma

cardiac, cardíaco

cardiologist, cardiólogo

cardiology, cardiología

care, cuidado

cartilage, cartílago

cast, yeso

castration, castración

cataract, catarata

catatonic, catatónico

catheter, catéter

catheterization, cateterismo

catheterize, cateterizar

cause, causa

cauterize, cauterizar

cervix, cuello del útero

chafe, rozar

checkup, examen

cheek, mejilla

chemical, químico

chemotherapy, quimioterapia

chest, pecho

chew, masticar

chicken pox, varicela

childbirth, parto

childhood, infancia

chills, escalofríos

chin, barbilla

chiropractor, quiropráctico

chlamydia, clamidia

choke, ahogarse

cholera, cólera

cholesterol, colesterol

chronic, crónico

cigarette, cigarrillo

circulation, circulación

circumcision, circuncisión

cirrhosis, cirrosis

claustrophobia, claustrofobia

cleft palate, paladar hendido

clinic, clínica

clitoris, clítoris

clot, coágulo

cocaine, cocaína

coccyx, cóccix

codeine, codeína

cold, frío/a

cold (illness), resfriado común

cold sores, herpes labial

colic, cólico

colitis, colitis

collagen, colágeno

collarbone, clavícula

colon, colon

colonoscopy, colonoscopía

color-blindness, daltonismo

colostomy, colostomia

coma, coma

comatose, comatoso

comfortable, cómodo

complaint, queja

complexion, tez

complication, complicación

compress, compresa

conceive, concebir

concussion, conmoción cerebral

condom, condón

confused, confundido

confusion, confusión

congenital, congénito

congested (to be), estar congestionado

congestion, congestión

conjunctiva, conjuntiva

conjunctivitis, conjuntivitis

conscious, consciente

consciousness, conocimiento

consent, consentir

constipation, estreñimiento

contagious, contagioso

contaminated, contaminado

contraception, anticoncepción

contractions, contracciones

contusion, contusión

convalescent, convaleciente

convulsion, convulsión

corn (callus), callo

coronary, coronario

cortisone, cortisona

cough, tos

cough, toser

CPR, reanimación cardiopulmonar

crabs, ladillas

cramp, calambre

cramps (menstrual), cólicos menstruales

cranium, cráneo

craving, antojo

crawl, gatear

crib, cuna

cripple, lisiar

crippled, lisiado

critical, crítico

Crohn's disease, enfermedad de Crohn

cross-eyed, bizco

croup, crup

crutches, muletas

cry, llorar

CT scan, tomografía por computadora

culture, cultivo

cure, curar

cut, cortar

cuticle, cutícula

cyst, quiste

cystic fibrosis, fibrosis quística

D

daily, diariamente

dandruff, caspa

danger, peligro

daze, aturdimiento

dead, muerto

deaf, sordo

deaf-mute, sordomudo

deafness, sordera

death, muerte

deceased, difunto

decongestant, descongestionante

defecate, defecar

defibrillation, desfibrilación

defibrillator, desfibrilador

deficiency, deficiencia

deformed, deformado

deformity, deformidad

dehydration, deshidratación

delirious, delirante

delirium, delirio

delivery (of a baby), parto

deltoids, deltoides

dementia, demencia

dental, dental

dentist, dentista

denture, dentadura postiza

depigmentation, despigmentación

depression, depresión

dermatitis, dermatitis

dermatologist, dermatólogo

deterioration, deterioro

detoxification, desintoxicación

develop, desarrollar

diabetes, diabetes

diagnose, diagnosticar

diagnosis, diagnóstico

dialysis, diálisis

diaper, pañal

diaphragm, diafragma

diarrhea, diarrea

die, morir

diet, dieta

dietitian, dietista

digest, digerir

digestion, digestión

dilated, dilatado

dilation, dilatación

dilute, diluir

diphtheria, difteria

disability, discapacidad

discharge, secreción

discharge from hospital, dar de alta

discontinue, suspender

disease, enfermedad

disinfect, desinfectar

disinfectant, desinfectante

disk (slipped), disco desplazado

dislocation, dislocación

disorder, trastorno

disorientation, desorientación

distend, distender

distressed, angustiado

diuretic, diurético

dizziness, mareos

dizzy, mareado

doctor, médico

doctor's office, consultorio

donor, donante

dosage, dosis

double vision, vista doble

drain, supurar

draw blood, sacar sangre

dropper, gotero

drops, gotas

drowning, ahogamiento

drowsy, somnoliento

drug addiction, adicción a las drogas

drugs (usually illicit), drogas

drugs (legal), medicinas

drunk, borracho

dryness, sequedad

due date, fecha aproximada de parto

dull (pain), sordo (dolor)

duodenum, duodeno

dust, polvo

dwarfism, enanismo

dysentery, disentería

dyslexia, dislexia

dystrophy, distrofia

E

ear (inner), oído

ear (middle), oído medio

ear (outer), oreja

earache, dolor de oído

eardrum, tímpano

earlobe, lóbulo

earplugs, tapones para los oídos

eczema, eccema

edema, edema

egg, huevo/óvulo

ejaculate, eyacular

EKG, electrocardiograma

elbow, codo

elderly, anciano

electrocardiogram, electrocardiograma

electrocution, electrocución

elixir, elixir

emaciated, escuálido

embolism, embolia

embryo, embrión

emergency, emergencia

pulmonary emphysema, enfisema pulmonar

encephalitis, encefalitis

endemic, endémico

endocrine, endocrino

endocrinologist, endocrinólogo

endorphin, endorfina

endoscopy, endoscopía

enema, enema

enlargement, agrandamiento

enzyme, enzima

epidemic, epidémico/epidemia

epidural, epidural

epiglottis, epiglotis

epilepsy, epilepsia

erection, erección

esophagus, esófago

estrogen, estrógeno

ether, éter

euphoria, euforia

Eustachian tube, trompa de Eustaquio

euthanasia, eutanasia

exam, examen

examine, examinar

excrement, excremento

exercise, ejercicio

exertion, esfuerzo

exfoliation, exfoliación

exhale, exhalar

exhaustion, agotamiento

expectorant, expectorante

expert, experto

explain, explicar

exposure, exposición

external, externo

extract, extraer

extraction, extracción

eye, ojo

eyebrow, ceja

eyelash, pestaña

eyelid, párpado

eyesight, vista

F

face, cara

face down, boca abajo

face up, boca arriba

faint, desmayarse

fainting spells, desmayos

fall, caída

Fallopian tubes, trompas de Falopio

false teeth, dientes postizos

family planning, planificación familiar

fast, ayunar

fat (food), grasa

fat (person), gordo

fatal, fatal/mortal

fatigue, fatiga

fear, miedo

feces, heces

feed, alimentar

feel, sentir

feet, pies

femur, fémur

fertile, fértil

fertilization, fertilización

fetal monitor, monitor fetal

fetus, feto

fever, fiebre

fiber, fibra

fibrillation, fibrilación

filling (dental), empaste

finger, dedo (de la mano)

finger pad, yema

fire, fuego/incendio

first aid, primeros auxilios

fissure, fisura

fist, puño

flake, escama

flat foot, pie plano

flatulence, flatulencia

flexible, flexible

flu, gripe

fluoride, fluoruro

flush, rubor

foam, espuma

folic acid, ácido fólico

folk healer, curandero

follicle, folículo

follow-up, examen de seguimiento

food, alimentos

foot, pie

forceps, fórceps

forearm, antebrazo

forehead, frente

foreskin, prepucio

form, formulario

formula, fórmula

fracture, fractura

freckle, peca

freeze, congelar

frequency, frecuencia

fright, susto

function, función

fungus, hongo

G

gag, provocar náuseas

gain weight, subir de peso

gall bladder, vesícula biliar

gallstones, cálculos biliares

gangrene, gangrena

gargle, hacer gárgaras

gas, gas

gash, tajo

gastric ulcer, úlcera gástrica

gastritis, gastritis

gastroenterologist, gastroenterólogo

gastrointestinal (GI), gastrointestinal

gauze, gasa

gel, gel

gender, sexo

genes, genes

genetic, genético

genitals, genitales

geriatric, geriátrico

germ, germen

German measles, rubéola

gestation, gestación

gigantism, gigantismo

giardia, giardia

gingivitis, gingivitis

gland, glándula

glasses, gafas

glaucoma, glaucoma

glove, guante

glucose, glucosa

gluten, gluten

goiter, bocio

gonorrhea, gonorrea

goose bumps, piel de gallina

gout, gota

gown, bata

graft, injerto

gram, gramo

grief, pesar

grieve, afligirse

grind, moler

groin, ingle

growth, crecimiento

guilt, culpa

gums, encías

gun, pistola

gurney, camilla

gut, intestino/tripas

gynecologist, ginecólogo

gynecology, ginecología

H

habit, hábito

hair, pelo

hair (body), vello

halitosis, mal aliento

hallucination, alucinación

hammer, martillo de reflejos

hamstring, músculo posterior del muslo

hand, mano

hangnail, padrastro

hangover, resaca

hardening, endurecimiento

harm, dañar

harmful, dañino

harmless, inofensivo

head, cabeza

headache, dolor de cabeza

heal, curarse

health, salud

health care, atención a la salud

healthy, sano

hear, oír

hearing, audición

heart, corazón

heart attack, ataque cardíaco

heartbeat, latido del corazón

heartburn, acidez estomacal

heat-stroke, insolación

heating pad, cojín eléctrico

heel, talón

height, altura

helicopter, helicóptero

hematoma, hematoma

hemoglobin, hemoglobina

hemophilia, hemofilia

hemorrhage, hemorragia

hepatitis, hepatitis

herb, hierba

herbalist, yerbero

hereditary, hereditario

heredity, herencia

hermaphrodite, hermafrodita

hernia, hernia

heroin, heroína

herpes, herpes

heterosexual, heterosexual

hiccups, hipo

high blood pressure, presión alta

hip, cadera

hives, ronchas

hoarse, ronco

hoarseness, ronquera

homeopathy, homeopatía

homosexual, homosexual

hookworm, anquilostomosis

hormonal, hormonal

hormone, hormona

hospital, hospital

hospitalize, internar

hot flashes, sofocos

hunchback, jorobado

hurt, doler

hydrate, hidratar

hydrogen peroxide, peróxido de hidrógeno

hygiene, higiene

hymen, himen

hyperactive, hiperactivo

hyperglycemia, hiperglucemia

hypersensitivity, hipersensibilidad

hypertension, presión alta

hyperthermia, hipertermia

hyperthyroidism, hipertiroidismo

hyperventilation, hiperventilación

hypochondria, hipocondria

hypoglycemia, hipoglucemia

hypothalamus, hipotálamo

hypothermia, hipotermia

hypothyroidism, hipotiroidismo

hypoxia, hipoxia

hysterectomy, histerectomía

hysteria, histeria

I

ibuprofen, ibuprofeno

ill, enfermo

illness, enfermedad

immature, inmaduro

immobile, inmóvil

immobilization, inmovilización

immune, inmune

immunize, inmunizar

impacted tooth, diente impactado

impaired, dañado

impairment, incapacidad

implant, implantar

impotence, impotencia

impregnation, fecundación

incest, incesto

incision, incisión

incontinence, incontinencia

incubator, incubadora

incurable, incurable

indigestion, indigestión

induce, inducir

infant, bebé

infect, infectar

infection, infección

infertile, estéril

infertility, infertilidad

inflammation, inflamación

influenza, gripe

ingest, ingerir

inhale, inhalar

inhaler, inhalador

inject, inyectar

injury, lesión

inoculate, inocular

inoculation, inoculación

insane, loco

insanity, locura

insemination, inseminación

insomnia, insomnio

instrument, instrumento

insulin, insulina

insurance, seguro

intensive care, terapia intensiva

intercourse, relaciones sexuales

internal, interno

internist, internista

intestine, intestino

intoxication, intoxicación

intravenous fluids, líquidos intravenosos

intubation, intubación

iodine, yodo

iron, hierro

irregular heartbeat, latidos cardíacos irregulares

irrigate, irrigar

irritation, irritación

itch, comezón

J

jaundice, ictericia/piel amarilla

jaw, mandíbula

jelly, jalea

jock itch, tiña crural

joint, articulación

jugular, yugular

juice, jugo

K

kidney, riñón

kidney failure, insuficiencia renal

kidney stones, cálculos renales

knee, rodilla

kneecap, rótula

knife, cuchillo

knot, nudo

knuckle, nudillo

L

labor, trabajo de parto

labor pains, dolores de parto

laboratory, laboratorio

labyrinthitis, laberintitis

laceration, laceración

lactation, lactancia

lactose, lactosa

lame extremity, extremidad lisiada

language, lenguaje

laparoscopy, laparoscopía

large intestine, intestino grueso

laryngitis, laringitis

larynx, laringe

laser treatment, tratamiento con láser

latex, látex

laughing gas, gas hilarante (óxido nitroso)

laxative, laxante

lead, plomo

leech, sanguijuela

left-handed, zurdo

leg, pierna

leprosy, lepra

lesbian, lesbiana

lesion, lesión

lethargy, letargo

leukemia, leucemia

libido, deseo sexual

lice, piojos

life, vida

lifestyle, estilo de vida

ligament, ligamento

light-headedness, vahído

limb, extremidad

liniment, linimento

liposuction, liposucción

lips, labios

liquid, líquido

lisp, ceceo

listen, escuchar

live, vivir

liver, hígado

lobe, lóbulo

lobotomy, lobotomía

lockjaw, tétanos

low blood pressure, presión baja

lozenges, pastillas para la garganta

lubricate, lubricar

lump, bulto

lumpectomy, tumorectomía

lungs, pulmones

lupus, lupus

lymph, linfa

lymph nodes, ganglios linfáticos

lymphoma, linfoma

M

malabsorption, malabsorción

malaise, malestar

malaria, paludismo

male, varón/masculino

malformation, malformación

malignant, maligno

malnutrition, desnutrición

malpractice, negligencia médica

mammogram, mamografía

mania, manía

manic-depressive, maníaco depresivo

marijuana, marihuana

mask, máscara

mass, masa

massage/rub, masajear

mastectomy, mastectomía

maternal, materno

maturity, madurez

measles, sarampión

medical record, expediente médico

medication, medicamento

medicine, medicina

melanoma, melanoma

meningitis, meningitis

menopause, menopausia

menses, menstruación

menstrual cycle, ciclo menstrual

menstruation, menstruación

mental illness, trastorno mental

metabolism, metabolismo

metastasis, metástasis

methadone, metadona

methamphetamine, metanfetamina

microscope, microscopio

microsurgery, microcirugía

midwife, partera

migraine, migraña

mind, mente

miscarriage, aborto natural

mite, ácaro

mole, lunar

monitor, monitor

mononucleosis, mononucleosis

morgue, morgue

morphine, morfina

mortality, mortalidad

mouth, boca

mucous, mucoso/mucosa

mumps, paperas

muscle, músculo

mutation, mutación

mute, mudo

myopia, miopía

N

nail, uña

naked, desnudo

nap, siesta

nape, nuca

narcolepsy, narcolepsia

narcotic, narcótico

natural, natural

nausea, náuseas

navel, ombligo

nearsightedness, miopía

neck, cuello

needle, aguja

nerve, nervio

nervous, nervioso

neuralgia, neuralgia

neurologist, neurólogo

neurology, neurología

neurosis, neurosis

neurotic, neurótico

nicotine, nicotina

nightmare, pesadilla

nipple, pezón

nitroglycerine, nitroglicerina

normal, normal

nose, nariz

nostril, fosa nasal

nourishment, nutrición

numbness, adormecimiento

nurse, enfermera

nutrient, nutriente

nutrition, nutrición

nutritionist, nutricionista

O

obese, obeso

obesity, obesidad

obstetrician, obstetra

obstetrics, obstetricia

obstruction, obstrucción

occlusion, oclusión

odor, olor

office, consultorio

ointment, ungüento

oncologist, oncólogo

oncology, oncología

operate, operar

ophthalmologist, oftalmólogo,

optic, óptico

optometrist, optometrista

oral, oral

organ, órgano

orgasm, orgasmo

orthodontist, ortodoncista

orthopedics, ortopedia

orthopedist, ortopedista

osteoarthritis, osteoartritis

osteopath, osteópata

osteoporosis, osteoporosis

ovary, ovario

overdose, sobredosis

overweight, sobrepeso

ovulate, ovular

ovulation, ovulación

oxygen, oxígeno

P

pacemaker, marcapaso

pacifier, chupete

pain, dolor

pain reliever, calmante para el dolor

painful, doloroso

palate, paladar

pale, pálido

paleness, palidez

palpitations, palpitaciones

pancreas, páncreas

Pap smear, examen de Papanicolaou

paralysis, parálisis

paralyzed, paralítico

paramedic, paramédico

paranoia, paranoia

paraplegic, parapléjico

parasite, parásito

patch, parche

paternal, paterno

pathologist, patólogo

patient, paciente

pediatric, pediátrico

pediatrician, pediatra

pediatrics, pediatría

pelvis, pelvis

penetrate, penetrar

penicillin, penicilina

penis, pene

perforation, perforación

perspire, transpirar

pertussis, tos ferina

pharmacist, farmacéutico

pharmacy, farmacia

pharynx, faringe

phlegm, flema

phobia, fobia

phosphorus, fósforo

photosensitivity, fotosensibilidad

physical therapy, fisioterapia

physician, médico

pill, píldora

pillow, almohada

pimples, espinillas

placenta, placenta

plague, plaga

plaque, placa

plasma, plasma

platelets, plaquetas

pneumonia, pulmonía

podiatrist, podólogo

poison, veneno

polio, poliomielitis

pollen, polen

polyp, pólipo

pore, poro

postmenopausal, postmenopáusico

post-op, después de la operación

postpartum, posparto

potassium, potasio

pound, libra

powder, polvo

predispose, predisponer

preeclampsia, pre eclampsia

pregnancy, embarazo

pregnant, embarazada

premature birth, nacimiento prematuro

premenopausal, pre menopáusico

prenatal care, cuidado prenatal

prescribe, recetar

prescription, receta

pressure, presión

prevent, prevenir

prevention, prevención

procedure, procedimiento

proctologist, proctólogo

progesterone, progesterona

prognosis, pronóstico

prostate gland, próstata

protein, proteína

psoriasis, psoriasis

psychiatrist, psiquiatra

psychologist, psicólogo

psychosis, psicosis

psychotherapy, psicoterapia

psychotic, psicótico

puberty, pubertad

pubic hair, vello púbico

pulmonary, pulmonar

pulmonary edema, edema pulmonar

pulsating, pulsante

pulse, pulso

pump, bomba

pupil, pupila

pus, pus

Q

quadriceps, cuádriceps

quarantine, cuarentena

quinine, quinina

quota, cuota

R

rabies, rabia

radiation treatment, tratamiento de radiación

radiologist, radiólogo

radiology, radiología

radiotherapy, radioterapia

rape, violación

rash, erupción

reaction, reacción

reconstruct, reconstruir

recovery, recuperación

rectum, recto

redness, enrojecimiento

refill, rellenar

reflex, reflejo

reflux, reflujo

regurgitation, regurgitación

rehabilitate, rehabilitar

rehydrate, rehidratar

reject, rechazar

relapse, recaída

relationship (family), parentesco

relax, descansar

relief, alivio

remedy, remedio

renal failure, insuficiencia renal

replace, reemplazar

reproduce, reproducir

reproduction, reproducción

respirator, respirador

respiratory, respiratorio

rest, descansar

result, resultado

resuscitation, resucitación

retention, retención

retina, retina

revive, reanimarse

rheumatic fever, fiebre reumática

rheumatism, reumatismo

rhinoplasty, rinoplastia

rhythm method, método del ritmo

rib, costilla

rigidity, rigidez

rigor mortis, rigor mortis

risk, riesgo

rubella, rubéola

runny nose, secreción nasal

rupture, ruptura

S

safe, seguro

saline, salino

saliva, saliva

salmonella, salmonela

salt, sal

sample, muestra

sane, cuerdo

sanitary, sanitario

sanity, cordura

sarcoma, sarcoma

scab, costra

scabies, sarna

scald, escaldadura

scale, balanza

scalp, cuero cabelludo

scaly, escamoso

scar, cicatriz

scarlet fever, fiebre escarlatina

schizophrenia, esquizofrenia

sciatica, ciática

scissors, tijeras

scoliosis, escoliosis

scratch, rasguño

scream, grito

screen, examen de detección

scrotum, escroto

scurvy, escorbuto

sealant, sellador

seasickness, mareo (en un barco)

secrete, secretar

secretion, secreción

sedative, sedante

sedentary, sedentario

seizures, convulsiones

semen, semen

senile, senil

senility, senilidad

sensation, sensación

sensitive, sensible

sensitivity, sensibilidad

septum, tabique

serious, serio

serum, suero

severe, severo

sex, sexo

sexuality, sexualidad

shakes, temblores

sharp (pain), agudo (dolor)

shin, espinilla

shingles, herpes zoster

shiver, escalofríos

shiver, tiritar

shock, choque

shot, inyección

shoulder, hombro

shoulder blade, omóplato

sibling, hermano/hermana

sick, enfermo

sickness, enfermedad

side, lado

side effect, efecto secundario

sight, vista

sinus, seno paranasal

sinusitis, sinusitis

skeleton, esqueleto

skin, piel

skinny, flaco

skull, cráneo

sleep, dormir

sleeping pill, somnífero

sleepy, tener sueño

sling, cabestrillo

slip, resbalar

slipped disc, disco desplazado

sliver, astilla

slur, arrastrar las palabras

small intestine, intestino delgado

smallpox, viruela

smell, oler

smoke, fumar

snakebite, mordedura de serpiente

sneeze, estornudar

snore, roncar

soap, jabón

sober, sobrio

social worker, trabajador social

sodium, sodio

sole (of foot), planta del pie

sonogram, ecografía

sore, llaga

spasm, espasmo

specialist, especialista

specimen, muestra/espécimen

speculum, espéculo

speech pathologist, foniatra

sperm, esperma

spermicide, espermicida

sphincter, esfínter

spider bite, picadura de araña

spina bifida, espina bífida

spinal column, columna vertebral

spinal cord, médula espinal

spleen, bazo

splint, férula

splint, entablillar

splinter, astilla

sponge, esponja

spots, manchas

spotted fever, fiebre maculosa

sprain, torcedura

sprain, torcerse

sputum, esputo

stab, puñalada

stain, mancha

starvation, inanición

sterile, estéril

sterility, esterilidad

sterilize, esterilizar

sternum, esternón

steroid, esteroide

stethoscope, estetoscopio

stiff, rígido

stimulant, estimulante

sting, picadura de insecto

sting, picar

stirrup, estribo

stitches, puntos de suturas

stoma, estoma

stomach, estómago

stomach ache/pain, dolor de estómago

stool, excremento

strangle, estrangular

strength, fuerza

strep, estreptococo

stress, estrés

stretch mark, estría

stretcher, camilla

stroke, derrame cerebral

strong, fuerte

stuffy nose, nariz tapada

stupor, estupor

stutter, tartamudear

suffocation, sofocación

suicide, suicidio

sunburn, quemadura por el sol

sunstroke, insolación

suppository, supositorio

surgeon, cirujano

surgery, cirugía

surrogate mother, madre portadora

survive, sobrevivir

suture, sutura

swab, hisopo

swallow, tragar

sweat, sudor

swelling, hinchazón

swollen, hinchado

symptom, síntoma

syndrome, síndrome

synthetic, sintético

syphilis, sífilis

syringe, jeringa

syrup, jarabe

T

table, mesa

tablespoonful, cucharada

tablet, tableta

tailbone, cóccix

take, tomar

talcum powder, talco

tampon, tampón

tapeworm, teniasis

taste, sabor

taste bud, papila gustativa

tattoo, tatuaje

tear (of muscle/ligament), desgarro

tear (of the eye), lágrima

teaspoonful, cucharadita

technician, técnico

temperature, temperatura

temple (of the head), sien

temporary, temporal

tender, adolorido

tendinitis, tendinitis

tendon, tendón

terminal, terminal

test, prueba/examen

testicles, testículos

testosterone, testosterona

tetanus, tétano

therapist, terapeuta

therapy, terapia

thermometer, termómetro

thick, espeso (consistency)/grueso (dimension)

thigh, muslo

thirst, sed

thirsty (to be), tener sed

thorax, tórax

throat, garganta

throbbing, pulsante

thrombosis, trombosis

throw up, vomitar

thumb, pulgar

thyroid gland, glándula tiroides

tincture, tintura

tingling, hormigueo

tinnitus, zumbido en los oídos

tissue, tejido

tobacco, tabaco

toe, dedo del pie

toilet, inodoro

tolerate, tolerar

tongue, lengua

tonic, tónico

tonsil, amígdala

tonsillectomy, amigdalectomía

tonsillitis, amigdalitis

tooth, diente

toothache, dolor de muelas

touch, tocar

tourniquet, torniquete

towel, toalla

toxemia, toxemia

toxic, tóxico

toxin, toxina

trace, rastro

trachea, traquea

traction, tracción

tranquilizers, tranquilizantes

transfusion, transfusión

transmitted, transmitido

transplant, trasplantar

trauma, trauma

traumatic, traumático

treat, tratar

treatment, tratamiento

tremors, temblores

triceps, tríceps

trouble, molestia

tube, tubo

tuberculosis, tuberculosis

tumor, tumor

tweezers, pinzas

twin, gemelo

twisted, torcido

typhoid fever, fiebre tifoidea

typhus, tifus

U

ulcer, úlcera

ultrasound, ultrasonido

umbilical cord, cordón umbilical

uncomfortable, incómodo

unconscious, inconsciente

unhealthy, insalubre

unstable, inestable

urethra, uretra

urgent, urgente

urinal, orinal

urinalysis, examen general de orina

urinary, urinario

urinate, orinar

urine, orina

urine sample, muestra de orina

urologist, urólogo

urology, urología

uterus, útero

V

vaccinate, vacunar

vaccine, vacuna

vagina, vagina

vaginal, vaginal

vaginitis, vaginitis

valve, válvula

varicose vein, vena varicosa

vascular, vascular

vasectomy, vasectomía

vegetative, vegetativo

vein, vena

venereal disease, enfermedad venérea

venom, veneno

ventilator, ventilador

ventricle, ventrículo

vertebrae, vértebras

vertigo, vértigo

victim, víctima

virile, viril

virus, virus

vision, vista

visiting hours, horario de visita

vital, vital

vital organ, órgano vital

vital signs, signos vitales

vitamin, vitamina

vocal cord, cuerda vocal

vomit, vomitar

W

waist, cintura

waiting room, sala de espera

wake up, despertar

walker, andador

ward, sala

warning, aviso

wart, verruga

wash (to), lavar

water, agua

watery eyes, ojos llorosos

weak, débil

weakness, debilidad

wean, destetar

weary, fatigado

weigh, pesar

weight, peso

weight change, cambio de peso

wet nurse, nodriza

wheel chair, silla de ruedas

wheeze, sibilancia

wheeze, respirar con sibilancias

white blood cells, glóbulos blancos

whooping cough (pertussis), tos ferina

windpipe, tráquea

wisdom tooth, muela del juicio

womb, útero

worms (intestinal), lombrices

wound, herida

wrist, muñeca

X

x-rays, radiografías/rayos X

Y

yawn, bostezar

SPANISH-ENGLISH
ESPAÑOL-INGLÉS

A

abdomen, abdomen

abdominal, abdominal

aborto, abortion

aborto natural, miscarriage

abrasión/raspadura, abrasion

absceso, abscess

abstinencia, abstinence

abuso, abuse

ácaro, mite

accidente, accident

acetaminofén, acetaminophen

acidez estomacal, heartburn

ácido, acid

ácido fólico, folic acid

acné, acne

aconsejar, advise (to)

activo, active

adicción, addiction

adicción a las drogas, drug addiction

adicto, addict

adolescencia, adolescence

adolorido, tender

adoptar, adopt (to)

adormecimiento, numbness

adrenalina, adrenaline

adulto, adult

afligirse, grieve

agitación, agitation

agotamiento, exhaustion

agrandamiento, enlargement

agua, water

agudo, acute

agudo (dolor), sharp (pain)

aguja, needle

ahogamiento, drowning

ahogarse, choke

aire, air

alcoholismo, alcoholism

alergia, allergy

alérgico, allergic

aliento, breath

alimentar, feed

alimentos, food

alivio, relief

almohada, pillow

altura, height

alucinación, hallucination

amargo, bitter

ambulancia, ambulance

amenorrea, amenorrhea

amígdala, tonsil

amigdalectomía, tonsillectomy

amigdalitis, tonsillitis

aminoácido, amino acid

amnesia, amnesia

amniocentesis, amniocentesis

amoníaco, ammonia

amoratado, bruised

ampolla, blister

amputar, amputate (to)

analgésico, analgesic

análisis, analysis

anatomía, anatomy

anciano, elderly

andador, walker

anemia, anemia

anémico, anemic

anestesia, anesthesia

anestesiólogo, anesthesiologist

aneurisma, aneurysm/aneurism

anfetaminas, amphetamines

angiograma, angiogram

angioplastia, angioplasty

angustiado, distressed

ano, anus

anorexia, anorexia

anormal, abnormal

anquilostomosis, hookworm

ansiedad, anxiety

antebrazo, forearm

antiácido, antacid

antibiótico, antibiotic

anticoagulante, anticoagulant

anticoncepción, contraception

anticuerpos, antibodies

antidepresivo, antidepressant

antídoto, antidote

antihistamínico, antihistamine

antojo, craving

ántrax, anthrax

aorta, aorta

aparato ortopédico, brace

apatía, apathy

apendectomía, appendectomy

apendicitis, appendicitis

apetito, appetite

aplicador, applicator

apnea, apnea

arrastrar las palabras, slur

arritmia, arrhythmia

arteria, artery

articulación, joint

artritis, arthritis

asfixia, asphyxia

asma, asthma

asmático, asthmatic

astigmatismo, astigmatism

astilla, sliver

astilla, splinter

ataque cardíaco, heart attack

atención a la salud, health care

atrofia, atrophy

aturdimiento, daze

audición, hearing

autismo, autism

autopsia, autopsy

aviso, warning

axila, arm pit

ayunar, fast

B

babero, bib

bacteria, bacteria

balanza, scale

bañarse, bathe (to)

baño, bath

barbilla, chin

barbitúricos, barbiturates

bario, barium

bastón, cane

bata, gown

bazo, spleen

bebé, baby

bebé, infant

benigno, benign

bíceps, biceps

bicúspide, bicuspid

bilirrubina, bilirubin

bilis, bile

biológico, biological

biopsia, biopsy

bizco, cross-eyed

boca, mouth

boca abajo, face down

boca arriba, face up

bocio, goiter

bolsa amniótica, amniotic sac

bomba, pump

borracho, drunk

bostezar, yawn

botella, bottle

botulismo, botulism

brazo, arm

bronquitis, bronchitis

bulimia, bulimia

bulímico, bulimic

bulto, lump

bursitis, bursitis

C

cabestrillo, sling

cabeza, head

cadera, hip

caída, fall

calambre, cramp

calcificado, calcified

calcio, calcium

cálculos biliares, gallstones

cálculos renales, kidney stones

callo, callus

callo, corn (callus)

calmante para el dolor, pain reliever

caloría, calorie

calvicie, baldness

calvo, bald

cama, bed

cambio de peso, weight change

camilla, gurney

camilla, stretcher

cáncer, cancer

canceroso, cancerous

capilar, capillary

cápsula, capsule

cara, face

carbohidrato, carbohydrate

carcinogénico, carcinogenic

carcinoma, carcinoma

cardíaco, cardiac

cardiología, cardiology

cardiólogo, cardiologist

cartílago, cartilage

caspa, dandruff

castración, castration

catarata, cataract

catatónico, catatonic

catéter, catheter

cateterismo, catheterization

cateterizar, catheterize

causa, cause

cauterizar, cauterize

ceceo, lisp

ceguera, blindness

ceja, eyebrow

cerebro, brain

choque, shock

cicatriz, scar

ciclo menstrual, menstrual cycle

ciego, blind

cigarrillo, cigarette

cintura, waist

circulación, circulation

circuncisión, circumcision

cirrosis, cirrhosis

cirugía, surgery

cirujano, surgeon

cita, appointment

clamidia, chlamydia

claustrofobia, claustrophobia

clavícula, collarbone

clínica, clinic

clítoris, clitoris

coágulo, clot

cocaína, cocaine

cóccix, coccyx

cóccix, tailbone

codeína, codeine

codo, elbow

cojín eléctrico, heating pad

colágeno, collagen

cólera, cholera

colesterol, cholesterol

cólico, colic

cólicos menstruales, cramps (menstrual)

colitis, colitis

colon, colon

colonoscopía, colonoscopy

colostomia, colostomy

columna vertebral, backbone

columna vertebral, spinal column

coma, coma

comatoso, comatose

comezón, itch

cómodo, comfortable

complicación, complication

compresa, compress

concebir, conceive

condón, condom

conducta, behavior

confundido, confused

confusión, confusion

congelar, freeze

congénito, congenital

congestión, congestion

conjuntiva, conjunctiva

conjuntivitis, conjunctivitis

conmoción cerebral, concussion

conocimiento, consciousness

consciente, conscious

consentir, consent

consultorio, doctor's office

consultorio, office

contagioso, contagious

contaminado, contaminated

contracciones, contractions

contusión, contusion

convaleciente, convalescent

convulsión, convulsion

convulsiones, seizures

corazón, heart

cordón umbilical, umbilical cord

cordura, sanity

coronario, coronary

cortar, cut

cortisona, cortisone

costilla, rib

costra, scab

cráneo, cranium

cráneo, skull

crecimiento, growth

crítico, critical

crónico, chronic

crup, croup

cuádriceps, quadriceps

cuarentena, quarantine

cucharada, tablespoonful

cucharadita, teaspoonful

cuchillo, knife

cuello, neck

cuello del útero, cervix

cuerda vocal, vocal cord

cuerdo, sane

cuero cabelludo, scalp

cuerpo, body

cuidado, care

cuidado prenatal, prenatal care

culpa, guilt

cultivo, culture

cuna, crib

cuota, quota

curandero, folk healer

curar, cure

curarse, heal

curita, bandaid

cutícula, cuticle

CH

chupete, pacifier

ciática, sciatica

D

daltonismo, color-blindness

dañado, impaired

dañar, harm

dañino, harmful

dar de alta, discharge from hospital

débil, weak

debilidad, weakness

dedo (de la mano), finger

dedo del pie, toe

defecar, defecate

deficiencia, deficiency

deformado, deformed

deformidad, deformity

delirante, delirious

delirio, delirium

deltoides, deltoids

demencia, dementia

dentadura postiza, denture

dental, dental

dentista, dentist

depresión, depression

dermatitis, dermatitis

dermatólogo, dermatologist

derrame cerebral, stroke

desarrollar, develop

descansar, relax

descansar, rest

descongestionante, decongestant

deseo sexual, libido

desfibrilación, defibrillation

desfibrilador, defibrillator

desgarro, tear (of muscle/ligament)

deshidratación, dehydration

desinfectante, disinfectant

desinfectar, disinfect

desintoxicación, detoxification

desmayarse, faint

desmayos, fainting spells

desnudo, naked

desnutrición, malnutrition

desorientación, disorientation

despertar, awaken (to)

despertar, wake up

despierto, awake

despigmentación, depigmentation

después de la operación, post-op

destetar, wean

deterioro, deterioration

diabetes, diabetes

diafragma, diaphragm

diagnosticar, diagnose

diagnóstico, diagnosis

diálisis, dialysis

diariamente, daily

diarrea, diarrhea

diente, tooth

diente impactado, impacted tooth

dientes postizos, false teeth

dieta, diet

dietista, dietitian

difteria, diphtheria

difunto, deceased

digerir, digest

digestión, digestion

dilatación, dilation

dilatado, dilated

diluir, dilute

discapacidad, disability

disco desplazado, disk (slipped)

disco desplazado, slipped disc

disentería, dysentery

dislexia, dyslexia

dislocación, dislocation

distender, distend

distrofia, dystrophy

diurético, diuretic

doler, hurt

dolor, ache

dolor, pain

dolor de cabeza, headache

dolor de estómago, stomach ache/pain

dolor de muelas, toothache

dolor de oído, earache

dolores de parto, labor pains

doloroso, painful

donante, donor

dormir, sleep

dosis, dosage

drogas, drugs (usually illicit)

duodeno, duodenum

E

eccema, eczema

ecografía, sonogram

edema, edema

edema pulmonar, pulmonary edema

efecto secundario, side effect

ejercicio, exercise

electrocardiograma, EKG

electrocardiograma, electrocardiogram

electrocución, electrocution

elixir, elixir

embarazada, pregnant

embarazo, pregnancy

embolia, embolism

embrión, embryo

emergencia, emergency

empaste, filling (dental)

enanismo, dwarfism

encamado, bedridden (patient)

encefalitis, encephalitis

encías, gums

endémico, endemic

endocrino, endocrine

endocrinólogo, endocrinologist

endorfina, endorphin

endoscopía, endoscopy

endurecimiento, hardening

enema, enema

enfermedad, ailment

enfermedad, disease

enfermedad, illness

enfermedad, sickness

enfermedad de Crohn, Crohn's disease

enfermedad venérea, venereal disease

enfermera, nurse

enfermo, ill

enfermo, sick

enfisema pulmonar, pulmonary emphysema

enojo, anger

enrojecimiento, redness

entablillar, splint

enuresis, bed-wetting

enzima, enzyme

epidémico/epidemia, epidemic

epidural, epidural

epiglotis, epiglottis

epilepsia, epilepsy

equilibrio, balance

erección, erection

eructar, burp

eructo, belch

erupción, rash

escaldadura, scald

escalofríos, chills

escalofríos, shiver

escama, flake

escamoso, scaly

escoliosis, scoliosis

escorbuto, scurvy

escroto, scrotum

escuálido, emaciated

escuchar, listen

esfínter, sphincter

esfuerzo, exertion

esófago, esophagus

espalda, back

espasmo, spasm

especialista, specialist

espéculo, speculum

esperma, sperm

espermicida, spermicide

espeso (consistency)/grueso (dimension), thick

espina bífida, spina bifida

espinilla, shin

espinillas, blackheads

espinillas, pimples

esponja, sponge

espuma, foam

esputo, sputum

esqueleto, skeleton

esquizofrenia, schizophrenia

estar congestionado, congested (to be)

estéril, infertile

estéril, sterile

esterilidad, sterility

esterilizar, sterilize

esternón, breastbone

esternón, sternum

esteroide, steroid

estetoscopio, stethoscope

estilo de vida, lifestyle

estimulante, stimulant

estoma, stoma

estómago, stomach

estornudar, sneeze

estrangular, strangle

estreñimiento, constipation

estreptococo, strep

estrés, stress

estría, stretch mark

estribo, stirrup

estrógeno, estrogen

estupor, stupor

éter, ether

euforia, euphoria

eutanasia, euthanasia

examen, checkup

examen, exam

examen de detección, screen

examen de Papanicolaou, Pap smear

examen de seguimiento, follow-up

examen general de orina, urinalysis

examinar, examine

excremento, excrement

excremento, stool

exfoliación, exfoliation

exhalar, exhale

expectorante, expectorant

expediente médico, medical record

experto, expert

explicar, explain

exposición, exposure

externo, external

extracción, extraction

extraer, extract

extremidad, limb

extremidad lisiada, lame extremity

eyacular, ejaculate

F

faringe, pharynx

farmacéutico, pharmacist

farmacia, pharmacy

fatal/mortal, fatal

fatiga, fatigue

fatigado, weary

fecha aproximada de parto, due date

fecundación, impregnation

fémur, femur

fértil, fertile

fertilización, fertilization

férula, splint

feto, fetus

fibra, fiber

fibrilación, fibrillation

fibrosis quística, cystic fibrosis

fiebre, fever

fiebre escarlatina, scarlet fever

fiebre maculosa, spotted fever

fiebre reumática, rheumatic fever

fiebre tifoidea, typhoid fever

fisioterapia, physical therapy

fisura, fissure

flaco, skinny

flatulencia, flatulence

flema, phlegm

flexible, flexible

fluoruro, fluoride

fobia, phobia

folículo, follicle

foniatra, speech pathologist

fórceps, forceps

fórmula, formula

formulario, form

fosa nasal, nostril

fósforo, phosphorus

fotosensibilidad, photosensitivity

fractura, fracture

frecuencia, frequency

frenos dentales, braces (dental)

frente, forehead

frío/a, cold

fuego/incendio, fire

fuerte, strong

fuerza, strength

fumar, smoke

función, function

G

gafas, glasses

ganglios linfáticos, lymph nodes

gangrena, gangrene

garganta, throat

gas, gas

gas hilarante (óxido nitroso), laughing gas

gasa, gauze

gastritis, gastritis

gastroenterólogo, gastroenterologist

gastrointestinal, gastrointestinal (GI)

gatear, crawl

gel, gel

gemelo, twin

genes, genes

genético, genetic

genitales, genitals

geriátrico, geriatric

germen, germ

gestación, gestation

giardia, giardia

gigantismo, gigantism

ginecología, gynecology

ginecólogo, gynecologist

gingivitis, gingivitis

glándula, gland

glándula tiroides, thyroid gland

glaucoma, glaucoma

glóbulos blancos, white blood cells

glucosa, glucose

gluten, gluten

glúteo, buttock

gonorrea, gonorrhea

gordo, fat (person)

gota, gout

gotas, drops

gotero, dropper

gramo, gram

grasa, fat (food)

Medical Vocabulary for Interpreters

gripe, flu

gripe, influenza

grito, scream

guante, glove

H

hábito, habit

hacer gárgaras, gargle

heces, feces

helicóptero, helicopter

hematoma, hematoma

hemofilia, hemophilia

hemoglobina, hemoglobin

hemorragia, hemorrhage

hepatitis, hepatitis

hereditario, hereditary

herencia, heredity

herida, wound

hermafrodita, hermaphrodite

hermano/hermana, sibling

hernia, hernia

heroína, heroin

herpes, herpes

herpes labial, cold sores

herpes zoster, shingles

heterosexual, heterosexual

hidratar, hydrate

hierba, herb

hierro, iron

hígado, liver

higiene, hygiene

himen, hymen

hinchado, swollen

hinchazón, swelling

hiperactivo, hyperactive

hiperglucemia, hyperglycemia

hipersensibilidad, hypersensitivity

hipertermia, hyperthermia

hipertiroidismo, hyperthyroidism

hiperventilación, hyperventilation

hipo, hiccups

hipocondria, hypochondria

hipoglucemia, hypoglycemia

hipotálamo, hypothalamus

hipotermia, hypothermia

hipotiroidismo, hypothyroidism

hipoxia, hypoxia

hisopo, swab

histerectomía, hysterectomy

histeria, hysteria

hombro, shoulder

homeopatía, homeopathy

homosexual, homosexual

hongo, fungus

horario de visita, visiting hours

hormigueo, tingling

hormona, hormone

hormonal, hormonal

hospital, hospital

hueso, bone

huevo/óvulo, egg

I

ibuprofeno, ibuprofen

ictericia/piel amarilla, jaundice

implantar, implant

impotencia, impotence

inanición, starvation

incapacidad, impairment

incesto, incest

incisión, incision

incómodo, uncomfortable

inconsciente, unconscious

incontinencia, incontinence

incubadora, incubator

incurable, incurable

indigestión, indigestion

inducir, induce

inestable, unstable

infancia, childhood

infección, infection

infectar, infect

infertilidad, infertility

inflamación, inflammation

ingerir, ingest

ingle, groin

ingresar, admit (into hospital)

inhalador, inhaler

inhalar, inhale

injerto, graft

inmaduro, immature

inmóvil, immobile

inmovilización, immobilization

inmune, immune

inmunizar, immunize

inoculación, inoculation

inocular, inoculate

inodoro, toilet

inofensivo, harmless

insalubre, unhealthy

inseminación, insemination

insolación, heat-stroke

insolación, sunstroke

insomnio, insomnia

instrumento, instrument

insuficiencia renal, kidney failure

insuficiencia renal, renal failure

insulina, insulin

internar, hospitalize

internista, internist

interno, internal

intestino, bowel

intestino, intestine

intestino delgado, small intestine

intestino grueso, large intestine

intestino/tripas, gut

intoxicación, intoxication

intubación, intubation

inyección, shot

inyectar, inject

irrigar, irrigate

irritación, irritation

J

jabón, soap

jalea, jelly

jarabe, syrup

jeringa, syringe

jorobado, hunchback

juanete, bunion

jugo, juice

L

laberintitis, labyrinthitis

labios, lips

laboratorio, laboratory

laceración, laceration

lactancia, lactation

lactosa, lactose

ladillas, crabs

lado, side

lágrima, tear (of the eye)

laparoscopía, laparoscopy

laringe, larynx

laringitis, laryngitis

látex, latex

latido del corazón, heartbeat

latidos cardíacos irregulares, irregular heartbeat

lavar, wash (to)

laxante, laxative

lengua, tongue

lenguaje, language

lepra, leprosy

lesbiana, lesbian

lesión, injury

lesión, lesion

letargo, lethargy

leucemia, leukemia

libra, pound

ligamento, ligament

linfa, lymph

linfoma, lymphoma

linimento, liniment

liposucción, liposuction

líquido, liquid

líquidos intravenosos, intravenous fluids

lisiado, crippled

lisiar, cripple

llaga, sore

llorar, cry

lobotomía, lobotomy

lóbulo, earlobe

lóbulo, lobe

loco, insane

locura, insanity

lombrices, worms (intestinal)

lubricar, lubricate

lunar, birthmark

lunar, mole

lupus, lupus

M

madre portadora, surrogate mother

madurez, maturity

mal aliento, halitosis

malabsorción, malabsorption

malestar, malaise

malformación, malformation

maligno, malignant

malo(a), bad

mamografía, mammogram

mancha, stain

manchas, spots

mandíbula, jaw

manía, mania

maníaco depresivo, manic-depressive

mano, hand

marcapaso, pacemaker

mareado, dizzy

mareo (en un barco), seasickness

mareos, dizziness

marihuana, marijuana

martillo de reflejos, hammer

masa, mass

masajear, massage/rub

máscara, mask

mastectomía, mastectomy

masticar, chew

materno, maternal

medicamento, medication

medicina, medicine

medicinas, drugs (legal)

médico, doctor

médico, physician

médula espinal, spinal cord

mejilla, cheek

melanoma, melanoma

meningitis, meningitis

menopausia, menopause

menstruación, menses

menstruación, menstruation

mente, mind

mesa, table

metabolismo, metabolism

metadona, methadone

metanfetamina, methamphetamine

metástasis, metastasis

método del ritmo, rhythm method

microcirugía, microsurgery

microscopio, microscope

miedo, fear

migraña, migraine

miopía, myopia

miopía, nearsightedness

moler, grind

molestia, trouble

monitor, monitor

monitor fetal, fetal monitor

mononucleosis, mononucleosis

mordedura, bite

mordedura de serpiente, snakebite

moretón, bruise

morfina, morphine

morgue, morgue

morir, die

mortalidad, mortality

mucoso/mucosa, mucous

mudo, mute

muela del juicio, wisdom tooth

muerte, death

muerto, dead

muestra, sample

muestra de orina, urine sample

muestra/espécimen, specimen

muletas, crutches

muñeca, wrist

músculo, muscle

músculo posterior del muslo, hamstring

muslo, thigh

mutación, mutation

N

nacimiento prematuro, premature birth

nacimiento/parto, birth

narcolepsia, narcolepsy

narcótico, narcotic

nariz, nose

nariz tapada, stuffy nose

natural, natural

náuseas, nausea

negligencia médica, malpractice

nervio, nerve

nervioso, nervous

neuralgia, neuralgia

neurología, neurology

neurólogo, neurologist

neurosis, neurosis

neurótico, neurotic

nicotina, nicotine

nitroglicerina, nitroglycerine

nodriza, wet nurse

normal, normal

nuca, nape

nudillo, knuckle

nudo, knot

nutrición, nourishment

nutrición, nutrition

nutricionista, nutritionist

nutriente, nutrient

O

obesidad, obesity

obeso, obese

obstetra, obstetrician

obstetricia, obstetrics

obstrucción, blockage

obstrucción, obstruction

oclusión, occlusion

oftalmólogo, ophthalmologist

oído, ear (inner)

oído medio, ear (middle)

oír, hear

ojo, eye

ojos llorosos, watery eyes

oler, smell

olor, odor

ombligo, bellybutton

ombligo, navel

omóplato, shoulder blade

oncología, oncology

oncólogo, oncologist

operar, operate

óptico, optic

optometrista, optometrist

oral, oral

oreja, ear (outer)

órgano, organ

órgano vital, vital organ

orgasmo, orgasm

orina, urine

orinal, bedpan

orinal, urinal

orinar, urinate

ortodoncista, orthodontist

ortopedia, orthopedics

ortopedista, orthopedist

osteoartritis, osteoarthritis

osteópata, osteopath

osteoporosis, osteoporosis

ovario, ovary

ovulación, ovulation

ovular, ovulate

oxígeno, oxygen

P

paciente, patient

padrastro, hangnail

paladar, palate

paladar hendido, cleft palate

palangana, basin

palidez, paleness

pálido, pale

palpitaciones, palpitations

paludismo, malaria

páncreas, pancreas

pantorilla, calf (of leg)

pañal, diaper

paperas, mumps

papila gustativa, taste bud

parálisis, paralysis

paralítico, paralyzed

paramédico, paramedic

paranoia, paranoia

parapléjico, paraplegic

parásito, parasite

parche, patch

parentesco, relationship (family)

parpadear, blink

párpado, eyelid

partera, midwife

parto, childbirth

parto, delivery (of a baby)

pastillas para la garganta, lozenges

paterno, paternal

patólogo, pathologist

peca, freckle

pecho, chest

pecho/seno, breast/chest

pediatra, pediatrician

pediatría, pediatrics

pediátrico, pediatric

peligro, danger

pelo, hair

pelvis, pelvis

pene, penis

penetrar, penetrate

penicilina, penicillin

perforación, perforation

peróxido de hidrógeno, hydrogen peroxide

pesadilla, nightmare

pesar, grief

pesar, weigh

peso, weight

pestaña, eyelash

pezón, nipple

picadura, bite (insect)

picadura de araña, spider bite

picadura de insecto, sting

picar, sting

pie, foot

pie de atleta, athlete's foot

pie plano, flat foot

piel, skin

piel de gallina, goose bumps

pierna, leg

pies, feet

píldora, pill

pinzas, tweezers

piojos, lice

pistola, gun

placa, plaque

placenta, afterbirth

placenta, placenta

plaga, plague

planificación familiar, family planning

planta del pie, sole (of foot)

plaquetas, platelets

plasma, plasma

plomo, lead

podólogo, podiatrist

polen, pollen

poliomielitis, polio

pólipo, polyp

polvo, dust

polvo, powder

poro, pore

posparto, postpartum

postmenopáusico, postmenopausal

potasio, potassium

pre eclampsia, preeclampsia

pre menopáusico, premenopausal

predisponer, predispose

prepucio, foreskin

presión, pressure

presión alta, high blood pressure

presión alta, hypertension

presión baja, low blood pressure

prevención, prevention

prevenir, prevent

primeros auxilios, first aid

procedimiento, procedure

proctólogo, proctologist

progesterona, progesterone

pronóstico, prognosis

próstata, prostate gland

proteína, protein

protuberancia, bump

provocar náuseas, gag

prueba/examen, test

psicólogo, psychologist

psicosis, psychosis

psicoterapia, psychotherapy

psicótico, psychotic

psiquiatra, psychiatrist

psoriasis, psoriasis

pubertad, puberty

pulgar, thumb

pulmonar, pulmonary

pulmones, lungs

pulmonía, pneumonia

pulsante, pulsating

pulsante, throbbing

pulso, pulse

puntos de suturas, stitches

puñalada, stab

puño, fist

pupila, pupil

pus, pus

Q

quebrar, break

queja, complaint

quemadura, burn

quemadura por el sol, sunburn

químico, chemical

quimioterapia, chemotherapy

quinina, quinine

quiropráctico, chiropractor

quiste, cyst

R

rabia, rabies

radiografías/rayos X, x-rays

radiología, radiology

radiólogo, radiologist

radioterapia, radiotherapy

rasguño, scratch

rastro, trace

reacción, reaction

reanimación cardiopulmonar, CPR

reanimarse, revive

recaída, relapse

receta, prescription

recetar, prescribe

rechazar, reject

reconstruir, reconstruct

recto, rectum

recuperación, recovery

reemplazar, replace

reflejo, reflex

reflujo, reflux

regurgitación, regurgitation

rehabilitar, rehabilitate

rehidratar, rehydrate

relaciones sexuales, intercourse

rellenar, refill

remedio, remedy

reproducción, reproduction

reproducir, reproduce

resaca, hangover

resbalar, slip

resfriado común, cold (illness)

respirador, respirator

respirar, breathe

respirar con sibilancias, wheeze

respiratorio, respiratory

resucitación, resuscitation

resultado, result

retención, retention

retina, retina

reumatismo, rheumatism

riesgo, risk

rigidez, rigidity

rígido, stiff

rigor mortis, rigor mortis

rinoplastia, rhinoplasty

riñón, kidney

rodilla, knee

roncar, snore

ronchas, hives

ronco, hoarse

ronquera, hoarseness

roto, broken

rótula, kneecap

rozar, chafe

rubéola, German measles

rubéola, rubella

rubor, flush

ruptura, rupture

S

sabor, taste

sacar sangre, draw blood

sal, salt

sala, ward

sala de espera, waiting room

salino, saline

saliva, saliva

salmonela, salmonella

salud, health

sangrar, bleed

sangre, blood

sanguijuela, leech

sanitario, sanitary

sano, healthy

sarampión, measles

sarcoma, sarcoma

sarna, scabies

secreción, discharge

secreción, secretion

secreción nasal, runny nose

secretar, secrete

sed, thirst

sedante, sedative

sedentario, sedentary

seguro, insurance

seguro, safe

sellador, sealant

semen, semen

senil, senile

senilidad, senility

seno paranasal, sinus

sensación, sensation

sensibilidad, sensitivity

sensible, sensitive

sentir, feel

sequedad, dryness

serio, serious

severo, severe

sexo, gender

sexo, sex

sexualidad, sexuality

shock anafiláctico, anaphylactic

sibilancia, wheeze

sien, temple (of the head)

siesta, nap

sífilis, syphilis

signos vitales, vital signs

silla de ruedas, wheel chair

síndrome, syndrome

sintético, synthetic

síntoma, symptom

sinusitis, sinusitis

sobredosis, overdose

sobrepeso, overweight

sobrevivir, survive

sobrio, sober

sodio, sodium

sofocación, suffocation

sofocos, hot flashes

somnífero, sleeping pill

somnoliento, drowsy

sordera, deafness

sordo, deaf

sordo (dolor), dull (pain)

sordomudo, deaf-mute

subir de peso, gain weight

sudor, sweat

suero, serum

suicidio, suicide

supositorio, suppository

supurar, drain

suspender, discontinue

susto, fright

sutura, suture

T

tabaco, tobacco

tabique, septum

tableta, tablet

tajo, gash

talco, talcum powder

talón, heel

tampón, tampon

tapones para los oídos, earplugs

tartamudear, stutter

tatuaje, tattoo

técnico, technician

tejido, tissue

temblores, shakes

temblores, tremors

temperatura, temperature

temporal, temporary

tendinitis, tendinitis

tendón, tendon

tener sed, thirsty (to be)

tener sueño, sleepy

teniasis, tapeworm

terapeuta, therapist

terapia, therapy

terapia intensiva, intensive care

terminal, terminal

termómetro, thermometer

testículos, testicles

testosterona, testosterone

tétano, tetanus

tétanos, lockjaw

tez, complexion

tifus, typhus

tijeras, scissors

tímpano, eardrum

tintura, tincture

tiña crural, jock itch

tiritar, shiver

toalla, towel

tocar, touch

tolerar, tolerate

tomar, take

tomografía por computadora, CT scan

tónico, tonic

tórax, thorax

torcedura, sprain

torcerse, sprain

torcido, twisted

torniquete, tourniquet

tos, cough

tos ferina, pertussis

tos ferina, whooping cough (pertussis)

toser, cough

toxemia, toxemia

tóxico, toxic

toxina, toxin

trabajador social, social worker

trabajo de parto, labor

tracción, traction

tragar, swallow

tranquilizantes, tranquilizers

transfusión, transfusion

transmitido, transmitted

transpirar, perspire

traquea, trachea

tráquea, windpipe

trasplantar, transplant

trastorno, disorder

trastorno mental, mental illness

tratamiento, treatment

tratamiento con láser, laser treatment

tratamiento de radiación, radiation treatment

tratar, treat

trauma, trauma

traumático, traumatic

tríceps, triceps

trombosis, thrombosis

trompa de Eustaquio, Eustachian tube

trompas de Falopio, Fallopian tubes

tuberculosis, tuberculosis

tubo, tube

tumor, tumor

tumorectomía, lumpectomy

U

úlcera, ulcer

úlcera gástrica, gastric ulcer

ultrasonido, ultrasound

ungüento, ointment

uña, nail

uretra, urethra

urgente, urgent

urinario, urinary

urología, urology

urólogo, urologist

útero, uterus

útero, womb

V

vacuna, vaccine

vacuna de refuerzo, booster shot

vacunar, vaccinate

vagina, vagina

vaginal, vaginal

vaginitis, vaginitis

vahído, light-headedness

válvula, valve

varicela, chicken pox

varón/masculino, male

vascular, vascular

vasectomía, vasectomy

vegetativo, vegetative

vejiga, bladder

vello, hair (body)

vello púbico, pubic hair

vena, vein

vena varicosa, varicose vein

vendaje, bandage

veneno, poison

veneno, venom

ventilador, ventilator

ventrículo, ventricle

verruga, wart

vértebras, vertebrae

vértigo, vertigo

vesícula biliar, gall bladder

víctima, victim

vida, life

vientre, belly

violación, rape

viril, virile

viruela, smallpox

virus, virus

vista, eyesight

vista, sight

vista, vision

vista doble, double vision

vital, vital

vitamina, vitamin

vivir, live

vivo, alive

vomitar, throw up

vomitar, vomit

Y

yema, finger pad

yerbero, herbalist

yeso, cast

yodo, iodine

yugular, jugular

Z

zumbido, buzzing

zumbido en los oídos, tinnitus

zurdo, left-handed

ABOUT THE AUTHOR

For more than 25 years, José Luis Leyva has been a translator and interpreter in various technical areas. His vast experience in bilingualism has allowed him to interpret for Presidents, Latin American and US governors, ambassadors, CEO's, judges, prosecutors, forensic experts and healthcare professionals. He is also the author of other books, including technical terminology books of the *Essential Technical Terminology* series.

ACERCA DEL AUTOR

Durante más de 25 años, José Luis Leyva se ha desempeñado como intérprete y traductor en diversas áreas técnicas. Su amplia experiencia lingüística lo ha llevado a interpretar para Presidentes de la República, gobernadores latinoamericanos y estadounidenses, embajadores, presidentes de compañías transnacionales, jueces, fiscales, peritos y profesionales del cuidado de la salud. Es también autor de varias obras, entre las que se incluyen los libros de terminología técnica de la serie *Essential Technical Terminology*.

Made in the USA
Monee, IL
06 May 2021

67829160R00095